I0156436

The Basement

ISBN: 978-1-935256-76-2

Published by L'Edge Press
P.O. Box 1652
Boone, NC 28607

www.ingramcontent.com/pod-product-compliance
Lightning Source LLC
Chambersburg PA
CBHW031144090426
42738CB00008B/1212
* 9 7 8 1 9 3 5 2 5 6 7 6 2 *